word building

In the Garden

Word Building with Prefixes and Suffixes

Pam Scheunemann

Consulting Editor, Diane Craig, M.A./Reading Specialist

A Division of ABDO

ABDO
Publishing Company

visit us at www.abdopublishing.com

Published by ABDO Publishing Company, a division of ABDO, P.O. Box 398166, Minneapolis, Minnesota 55439. Copyright © 2013 by Abdo Consulting Group, Inc. International copyrights reserved in all countries. No part of this book may be reproduced in any form without written permission from the publisher. Super SandCastle™ is a trademark and logo of ABDO Publishing Company.

Printed in the United States of America, North Mankato, Minnesota
062012
092012

 PRINTED ON RECYCLED PAPER

Editor: Liz Salzmann
Content Developer: Nancy Tuminelly
Interior Design: Kelly Doudna, Mighty Media, Inc.
Production: Oona Gaarder-Juntti, Mighty Media, Inc.
Photo Credits: Brand X Pictures, Comstock Images, David Sacks, George Doyle, Hermera Technologies, IT Stock Free, Jupiterimages, Maria Teijeiro, Polka Dot images, Shutterstock, Stockbyte, Thinkstock Images

Library of Congress Cataloging-in-Publication Data
Scheunemann, Pam, 1955-
  In the garden : word building with prefixes and suffixes / Pam Scheunemann.
    p. cm. -- (Word building)
  ISBN 978-1-61714-967-2
  1. English language--Suffixes and prefixes--Juvenile literature. 2. Vocabulary--Juvenile literature. 3. Language arts (Elementary) I. Title.
  PE1175.S345 2012
  428.1--dc22
                              2010054483

Super SandCastle™ books are created by a team of professional educators, reading specialists, and content developers around five essential components—phonemic awareness, phonics, vocabulary, text comprehension, and fluency—to assist young readers as they develop reading skills and strategies and increase their general knowledge. All books are written, reviewed, and leveled for guided reading, early reading intervention, and Accelerated Reader® programs for use in shared, guided, and independent reading and writing activities to support a balanced approach to literacy instruction.

contents

What Is Word Building? 4

Let's Build Words . . . . , . . 6

Madison Grows a Lovely Garden 16

Match It Up! 22

Glossary 24

What is Word Building?

Word building is adding groups of letters to a word. The added letters change the word's meaning.

weeds

Prefix

Some groups of letters are added to the beginning of words. They are called prefixes. Some prefixes have more than one meaning.

Suffix

Some groups of letters are added to the end of words. They are called suffixes. Some suffixes have more than one meaning.

re + **weed** + ing

prefix + base word + suffix

reweeding

The prefix **re** means to do it again.
The base word **weed** means to remove unwanted plants.
The suffix **ing** means that the action is happening now.
Reweeding means someone is removing unwanted plants again.

Let's Build words

plant

Alex has some carrot seeds to plant.

Donna plants flower seeds.

Eric is replanting the sprout.

plants

The suffix **s** means that the action is happening now.

replanting

The prefix **re** means to do it again.

The suffix **ing** means that the action is happening now.

More Words

planted, planter, planters, replant, replants, transplant, transplants, transplanted, transplanting

water

Samantha waters the plant for her mother.

Ann's yellow flower went unwatered for weeks.

John is watering his garden.

waters

The suffix **s** means that the action is happening now.

unwater**ed**

The prefix **un** means not or opposite.

The suffix **ed** means that the action already happened.

water**ing**

The suffix **ing** means that the action is happening now.

More Words

watered, waterless, waterlessly, waterlessness, overwater, rewater

9

work

Lisa works in the garden with her gloves on.

A gardener uses a shovel to rework the soil.

works

The suffix **s** means that the action is happening now.

rework

The prefix **re** means to do something again.

working

The suffix **ing** means that the action is happening now.

More Words

worker, workers, workable, unworkable, reworks

Riley and her mom are working together in the garden.

use

Wendy likes to use the basket for her vegetables.

Jenna reuses the pink flowerpot from last year.

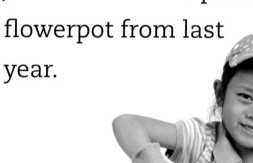

James is using the hose in the backyard.

reuses

The prefix **re** means to do it again.

The suffix **s** means that the action is happening now.

using

The suffix **ing** means that the action is happening now.

More words

uses, user, users, useful, usefully, useless, uselessly, uselessness, usefulness, useable, unusable, reused, reusable

ᷦᷦ ᷦ RULE ᷦ ᷦ ᷦ

When a verb ends with *e*, drop the *e* before adding **ing**.

13

rake

Daniel and Abby rake leaves on a fall day.

Carol is raking the front yard.

Isabella and Dean play in the unraked leaves.

raking

The suffix **ing** means that the action is happening now.

unraked

The prefix **un** means not or opposite.

The suffix **ed** turns a word into an adjective.

More Words

rakes, raker, rakers, raked

ꙮ ꙮ ꙮ RULE ꙮ ꙮ ꙮ

When a verb ends with e, drop the e before adding **ing** or **ed**.

Madison Grows a Lovely Garden

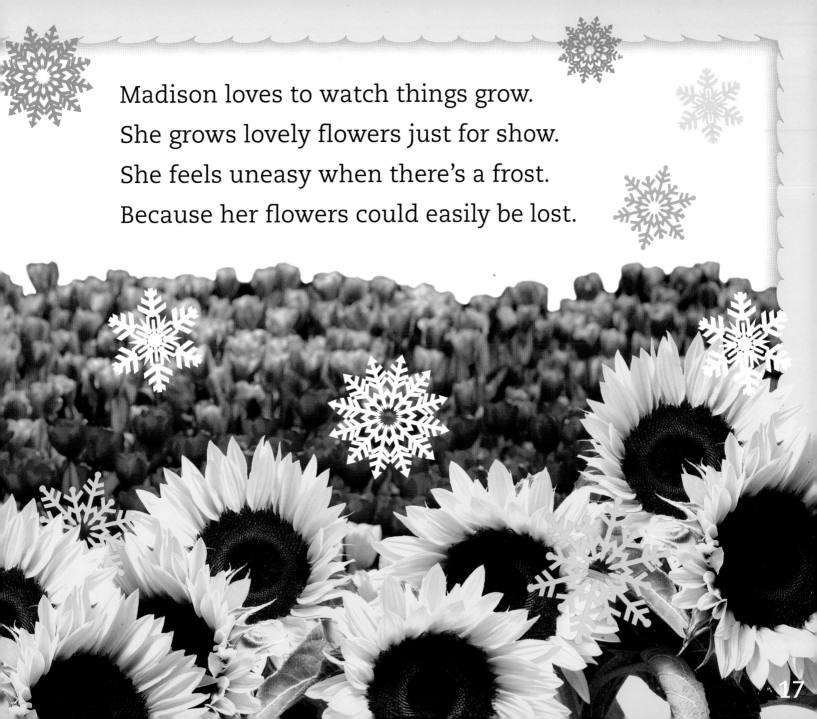

Madison loves to watch things grow.

She grows lovely flowers just for show.

She feels uneasy when there's a frost.

Because her flowers could easily be lost.

17

Madison plants her flowers
in a sunny spot.
She replants them in the
shade if they get too hot.
Watering just right is
an important job.
She learned not to overwater
from her best friend Bob.

Madison's garden was
unfenced until yesterday.
She fenced it in to keep
the deer away.
It's untrue that her garden
is made of gold.
But it truly is a sight
to behold!

Match It Up!

Choose the word with the correct prefix or suffix to complete each sentence.

1 Ashley is _____ the plants.

    a. waters

    b. watering

2 Jake just _____ a tree.

    a. replant

    b. planted

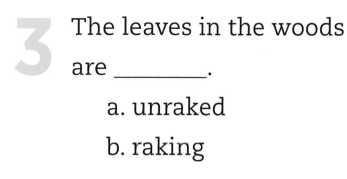

3 The leaves in the woods
are _____.

    a. unraked

    b. raking

4 Chris likes _____ in the garden.

    a. working

    b. reworked

5 Annie _____ new garden tools.

    a. reusing

    b. uses

Glossary

adjective (p. 15) – a word used to describe someone or something. Tall, green, round, happy, and cold are all adjectives.

behold (p. 20) – to see or look at something.

frost (p. 17) – a time when the outside temperature goes below freezing.

glove (p. 10) – a hand covering worn for decoration or protection.

hose (p. 13) – a long tube used to carry liquids such as water.

meaning (pp. 4, 5) – the idea or sense of something said or written.

opposite (pp. 9, 15) – being completely different from another thing.

sprout (p. 7) – a new plant growing from a seed.

uneasy (p. 17) – worried or uncomfortable.

verb (pp. 13, 15) – a word for an action. Be, do, think, play, and sleep are all verbs.

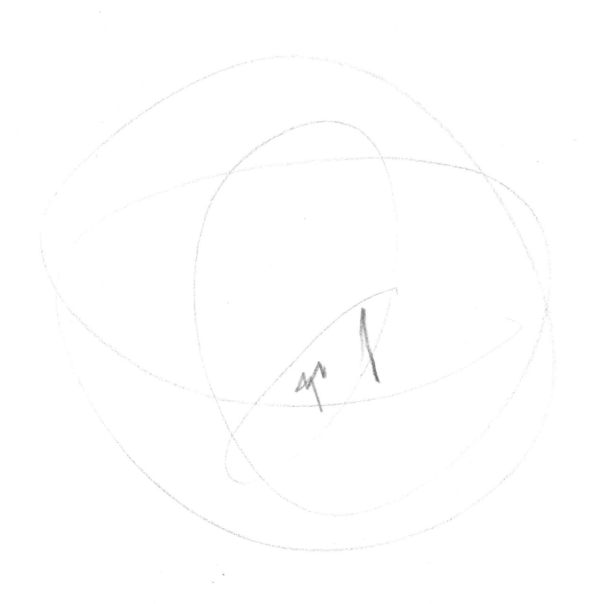